Unsettled Borders: Guyana-Venezuela and the Esequibo Oil-Rich Territory

Copyright Page

TITLE: Unsettled Borders: Guyana-Venezuela and the Esequibo Oil-Rich Territory

1ST Edition

Unsettled Borders: Guyana-Venezuela and the Esequibo Oil-Rich Territory

By Roberto Miguel Rodriguez

Book Outline

Introduction:

The Guyana-Venezuela border dispute and their claims over the Esequibo oil-rich territory have been ongoing for centuries. This subchapter provides a brief introduction to the book, outlining the proposed chapters and sub-chapters. It also emphasizes that the specific content and structure within each sub-chapter may vary based on the research and analysis conducted for the book.

Guyana-Venezuela Border Dispute and Their Claims Over the Esequibo Oil-Rich Territory:

This subchapter delves into the historical background of the border dispute, exploring the conflicting claims made by Guyana and Venezuela over the Esequibo oil-rich territory. It analyzes the roots of the dispute, including colonial history, treaties, and geopolitical factors.

Legal Aspects of the Guyana-Venezuela Border Dispute:

Here, we examine the legal aspects of the border dispute, including international law, treaties, and agreements that have shaped the conflicting claims. This subchapter also explores the role of international organizations and legal frameworks in resolving territorial disputes.

Environmental Impact of the Esequibo Oil-Rich Territory:

The Esequibo oil-rich territory is not only a source of economic potential but also home to unique ecosystems and biodiversity. This subchapter explores the environmental impact of exploration and exploitation of oil resources in the disputed area, highlighting the potential risks and challenges faced by the region.

Economic Implications of the Guyana-Venezuela Border Dispute:

The Guyana-Venezuela border dispute has significant economic implications for both countries. This subchapter examines the potential economic benefits and challenges of the Esequibo oil-rich territory, including the impact on national economies, investment opportunities, and resource management.

Geopolitical Factors Influencing the Border Dispute:

The border dispute between Guyana and Venezuela is not only a bilateral issue but also influenced by regional and global geopolitical factors. This subchapter analyzes the geopolitical dynamics at play, including the involvement of other nations and their interests in the dispute.

Social and Cultural Consequences of the Dispute on Affected Communities:

The border dispute has profound social and cultural consequences for the communities living in the disputed area. This subchapter explores the impact on local populations, including displacement, cultural heritage, and social tensions, shedding light on the human dimension of the dispute.

Exploration and Exploitation of Oil Resources in the Esequibo Territory:

This subchapter focuses on the exploration and exploitation of oil resources in the Esequibo territory. It examines the potential benefits and challenges associated with oil extraction, including environmental concerns, indigenous rights, and the role of multinational corporations.

International Mediation Efforts in Resolving the Border Dispute:

Efforts have been made to mediate and resolve the border dispute between Guyana and Venezuela. This subchapter explores the role of international mediation, including the involvement of organizations such as the United Nations and the Caribbean Community (CARICOM), and evaluates the prospects for a peaceful resolution.

Impact of the Border Dispute on Regional Stability and Relations between Guyana and Venezuela:

The border dispute has broader implications for regional stability and the bilateral relations between Guyana and Venezuela. This subchapter analyzes the impact of the dispute on regional dynamics, security concerns, and the potential for cooperation and conflict resolution.

Perspectives and Opinions from Local Residents and Stakeholders in the Disputed Area:

To provide a comprehensive understanding of the border dispute, this subchapter presents perspectives and opinions from local residents and stakeholders in the disputed area. It includes interviews, case studies, and personal stories, giving voice to those directly affected by the ongoing conflict.

Conclusion:

In conclusion, this book aims to provide a comprehensive analysis of the Guyana-Venezuela border dispute and their claims over the Esequibo oil-rich territory. By examining historical, legal, environmental, economic, geopolitical, social, and cultural aspects, it sheds light on the complexities and implications of this longstanding dispute. The book emphasizes that the specific content and structure within each sub-chapter may vary based on the research and analysis conducted for the book.

Guyana-Venezuela Border Dispute and Their Claims Over the Esequibo Oil-Rich Territory

Historical background of the Guyana-Venezuela border dispute

The historical background of the Guyana-Venezuela border dispute is a complex and contentious issue that has spanned over a century. This subchapter aims to provide an overview of the key events and factors that have shaped this dispute, shedding light on its historical context.

The origins of the border dispute can be traced back to the 19th century when Venezuela claimed sovereignty over the Essequibo region, an oil-rich territory administered by British Guiana (now Guyana). The dispute intensified in the early 20th century as oil discoveries in the Essequibo territory increased its strategic importance.

In 1899, an international tribunal, known as the Arbitral Award, was established to settle the dispute between Britain and Venezuela. The tribunal ruled in favor of Guyana, upholding the validity of the 1899 border agreement that established the boundary between the two countries. However, Venezuela refused to accept the decision and continued to claim the Essequibo territory.

Over the years, several attempts were made to resolve the dispute through diplomatic means, including negotiations and mediation efforts by various international actors. However, these efforts have been largely unsuccessful, with both countries maintaining their respective claims over the territory.

The border dispute has had significant legal implications, with both Guyana and Venezuela presenting their cases before international courts and tribunals. In 2018, the International Court of Justice (ICJ) ruled that it had jurisdiction to hear the case brought by Guyana, setting the stage for a final resolution of the dispute in the coming years.

The dispute also has environmental and economic implications. The Essequibo territory is believed to hold substantial oil reserves, making it a valuable resource for both countries. However, the exploration and exploitation of these resources have been hampered by the ongoing dispute, causing uncertainty and hindering investment in the region.

Furthermore, the border dispute has had social and cultural consequences for the affected communities living in the disputed area. Their lives have been disrupted by the uncertainty and tension surrounding the dispute, impacting their livelihoods and overall well-being.

The Guyana-Venezuela border dispute has also been influenced by geopolitical factors, with regional and international actors taking sides and exerting pressure on the involved parties. This has further complicated the resolution process and affected regional stability.

In conclusion, the historical background of the Guyana-Venezuela border dispute is a multifaceted issue that encompasses a range of factors. It is a dispute that has endured for over a century, with significant legal, environmental, economic, and social implications. Efforts to resolve the dispute have been ongoing, but a final resolution remains elusive. The perspectives and opinions of local residents and stakeholders in the disputed area are crucial in understanding the impact of this dispute on their lives and communities.

Early territorial claims and colonial influence

The origins of the Guyana-Venezuela border dispute can be traced back to the colonial era when European powers were vying for control over South America. In the 16th century, both Spain and Britain began establishing colonies in the region, which eventually led to conflicting territorial claims.

Spain, as a colonial power, asserted its authority over the entire continent, including what is now Guyana. However, the Dutch also had a significant presence in the area and established settlements along the Essequibo River, which became the focal point of the border dispute.

During the 19th century, as Venezuela gained independence from Spain, it inherited the territorial claims made by its former colonizer. Meanwhile, Britain continued to expand its influence in the region and eventually established control over what is now Guyana.

The conflicting claims between Venezuela and Britain escalated in the late 19th century, with Venezuela asserting that the border should follow the Essequibo River, while Britain argued for a border further to the east. This disagreement resulted in tension and diplomatic negotiations that lasted for decades.

Legal aspects also played a significant role in the border dispute. Both countries presented their cases to impartial international bodies, such as the Permanent Court of Arbitration in 1899. However, the arbitral award did not settle the dispute definitively, as Venezuela rejected the decision and maintained its claim over the Essequibo territory.

The environmental impact of the disputed territory cannot be overlooked. The Essequibo region is known for its rich biodiversity, including pristine rainforests, rivers, and unique ecosystems. The ongoing border dispute has hindered conservation efforts and sustainable development in the area, leading to concerns about deforestation, habitat destruction, and the loss of endangered species.

Furthermore, the economic implications of the border dispute are significant. The Essequibo territory is believed to hold substantial oil reserves, making it an attractive prospect for exploration and exploitation. However, the dispute has created uncertainty for potential investors, hindering the development of the oil industry in the region and depriving both countries of potential economic benefits.

The geopolitical factors influencing the border dispute are complex. Venezuela's historical rivalry with the United States and its desire to assert its regional influence have played a role in its stance on the dispute. Additionally, the strategic importance of the region for maritime trade and security has attracted attention from other global powers, further complicating the issue.

The social and cultural consequences of the dispute have been particularly felt by the communities living in the disputed area. These communities, both Guyanese and Venezuelan, have faced uncertainty, displacement, and restricted access to basic services. Their lives have been disrupted by the ongoing tensions and the lack of resolution to the dispute.

Efforts to mediate the border dispute have been made at the international level, with organizations such as the United Nations and the Caribbean Community (CARICOM) facilitating negotiations between the two countries. However, a lasting resolution has yet to be achieved, and the dispute continues to impact regional stability and relations between Guyana and Venezuela.

Local residents and stakeholders in the disputed area have diverse perspectives and opinions on the matter. Some argue for a peaceful resolution through dialogue and compromise, while others advocate for a more assertive approach to defending their country's territorial integrity. Their voices are crucial in understanding the human impact of the dispute and finding a solution that takes into account the needs and aspirations of those directly affected.

In conclusion, the early territorial claims and colonial influence have laid the foundation for the ongoing Guyana-Venezuela border dispute. The legal, environmental, economic, geopolitical, social, and cultural aspects of the dispute are intertwined and have wide-ranging implications for both countries and the region as a whole. Finding a resolution that addresses these complex issues is crucial for promoting stability, sustainable development, and harmonious relations between Guyana and Venezuela.

The Geneva Agreement of 1966 and its impact

The Geneva Agreement of 1966 marked a significant turning point in the Guyana-Venezuela border dispute and had wide-ranging impacts on various aspects of the conflict. This subchapter explores the agreement's provisions and its subsequent effects on the region.

Signed on February 17, 1966, the Geneva Agreement aimed to resolve the longstanding territorial dispute between Guyana and Venezuela over the Esequibo oil-rich territory. The agreement established a framework for negotiations and established a Mixed Commission comprised of representatives from both countries, as well as a neutral chairman appointed by the United Nations Secretary-General.

One of the most significant impacts of the Geneva Agreement was the formalization of the dispute resolution process. It provided a peaceful means for both countries to address their claims and counterclaims through dialogue and negotiation, thus avoiding armed conflict. This legal aspect of the agreement was crucial in maintaining regional stability and preventing the escalation of tensions.

The environmental impact of the Esequibo oil-rich territory was also a key concern addressed by the agreement. The disputed area is home to diverse ecosystems, including rainforests and rivers, which are vital for the region's biodiversity. The agreement mandated that both countries should refrain from disturbing the environment during exploration and exploitation activities, ensuring the preservation of these natural resources.

Moreover, the Geneva Agreement had significant economic implications for both Guyana and Venezuela. The Esequibo territory is believed to hold substantial oil reserves, potentially transforming the economy of the country that gains control over it. The agreement allowed for the continuation of exploration and exploitation activities by both countries, albeit under certain conditions, thereby enabling them to tap into the oil resources and potentially boost their economies.

The geopolitical factors influencing the border dispute were also addressed within the agreement. It recognized the importance of regional stability and the need for international mediation efforts. The agreement facilitated the engagement of various international actors, including the United Nations, in the resolution process, thereby ensuring that the dispute remained on the global agenda.

Furthermore, the social and cultural consequences of the dispute on affected communities were acknowledged by the Geneva Agreement. It emphasized the need to protect the rights of local residents and stakeholders in the disputed area, ensuring their voices were heard throughout the negotiation process.

In conclusion, the Geneva Agreement of 1966 played a vital role in shaping the Guyana-Venezuela border dispute and its subsequent impacts. By providing a legal framework for negotiations, addressing environmental concerns, considering economic implications, recognizing geopolitical factors, and safeguarding the rights of affected communities, the agreement laid the foundation for resolving the dispute through peaceful means and maintaining stability in the region.

Escalation of tensions in the 21st century

In the 21st century, the long-standing border dispute between Guyana and Venezuela over the Esequibo oil-rich territory has witnessed an alarming escalation of tensions. This subchapter aims to shed light on the various factors that have contributed to the intensification of this dispute, impacting not only the two countries involved but also the wider region.

Historically, the border dispute between Guyana and Venezuela can be traced back to the 19th century when Venezuela laid claim to the entire Essequibo region. However, it is in recent years that the dispute has taken a more aggressive turn. One of the primary reasons for this escalation is the discovery of vast oil reserves in the Esequibo territory. As oil becomes an increasingly valuable resource, both countries have intensified their efforts to secure ownership of the area.

From a legal perspective, the dispute has become more complex. Guyana maintains that the 1899 Arbitral Award settled the border issue, while Venezuela argues that this decision was invalid. This legal ambiguity has further fueled tensions between the two nations, with both sides steadfast in their claims.

The environmental impact of the dispute cannot be ignored. The Esequibo region is home to diverse ecosystems and rich biodiversity. The exploration and exploitation of oil resources in this area pose significant risks to the environment, including potential oil spills and habitat destruction. Such concerns have raised alarm bells among environmentalists and local communities, adding to the tensions surrounding the dispute.

Economically, the border dispute has implications for both Guyana and Venezuela. The potential revenue from the oil reserves in the Esequibo territory could significantly boost their economies. However, the uncertainty surrounding ownership has hindered investment and exploration efforts, stalling economic growth in the region.

Geopolitical factors have also influenced the escalation of tensions in the dispute. Both Guyana and Venezuela have sought support from international allies, further polarizing the issue. The involvement of external powers has complicated the resolution process and heightened regional tensions.

The social and cultural consequences of the border dispute cannot be overlooked. Communities living in the disputed area have been deeply affected, with their lives disrupted and their future uncertain. The dispute has strained relations between neighboring communities and has led to the displacement of many individuals.

International mediation efforts have been ongoing, but progress has been slow. The involvement of organizations such as the United Nations and the Caribbean Community (CARICOM) has attempted to find a peaceful resolution to the dispute. However, the stakes are high, and finding a compromise that satisfies both parties has proven challenging.

The impact of the border dispute on regional stability and relations between Guyana and Venezuela is significant. The tensions have strained diplomatic ties and hindered cooperation on various issues, including security and trade. The potential for a military confrontation looms, threatening peace and stability in the region.

To gain a deeper understanding of the dispute, it is essential to consider the perspectives and opinions of local residents and stakeholders in the disputed area. Their voices reveal the human aspect of the conflict, highlighting the profound impact it has on their lives and livelihoods.

In conclusion, the escalation of tensions in the 21st century in the Guyana-Venezuela border dispute over the Esequibo oil-rich territory has brought forth various intricate issues. From legal and environmental concerns to economic implications and geopolitical factors, the dispute has far-reaching consequences. As the dispute continues, it is crucial to explore possible avenues for resolution and consider the perspectives of those most affected by this ongoing conflict.

Legal aspects of the Guyana-Venezuela border dispute

The Guyana-Venezuela border dispute over the Esequibo oil-rich territory has a long and complex legal history. This subchapter aims to provide an overview of the legal aspects surrounding this contentious issue.

The dispute dates back to the colonial era when both Guyana and Venezuela were under Spanish rule. The Spanish crown granted the Essequibo region to the Dutch, who later transferred it to British control. However, Venezuela argues that the 1899 Arbitral Award, which established the border between the two nations, was invalid, claiming that it was a result of British manipulation.

The legal aspects of the border dispute have been examined by various international organizations, including the United Nations. In 1966, both countries agreed to refer the matter to the UN Secretary-General, who appointed a Good Offices process to facilitate negotiations between the two parties. The Good Offices process aimed to find a peaceful resolution based on international law and relevant treaties.

The primary legal framework for the dispute is the Geneva Agreement of 1966, which both countries signed. Under this agreement, the parties agreed to resolve the dispute through peaceful means, including negotiation, mediation, and arbitration. The Geneva Agreement also affirmed the validity of the 1899 Arbitral Award and established a Mixed Commission to oversee the resolution process.

Throughout the years, various legal arguments have been put forward by both Guyana and Venezuela. Guyana asserts that the 1899 Arbitral Award is final and binding, while Venezuela argues that it was null and void. Venezuela has also claimed that the Essequibo territory belongs to them based on historical, geographical, and legal grounds.

The legal aspects of the dispute have had significant implications for both countries. The uncertainty surrounding the border has hindered investment and development in the Esequibo oil-rich territory. It has also impacted regional stability and relations between Guyana and Venezuela, leading to occasional tensions and diplomatic disputes.

Efforts to resolve the dispute through international mediation have been ongoing. The United Nations Secretary-General has appointed various Special Representatives to facilitate negotiations between the two parties. However, a final resolution has yet to be reached.

Public opinion in the disputed area is divided, with stakeholders expressing different perspectives and opinions. Local residents and communities have been affected socially and culturally, as the dispute has disrupted their daily lives and economic activities.

In conclusion, the legal aspects of the Guyana-Venezuela border dispute are complex and have far-reaching implications. The dispute is rooted in historical and legal arguments, and efforts to find a resolution have involved international mediation and negotiation. The impact of the dispute extends beyond legal considerations, affecting regional stability, economic development, and the lives of communities in the disputed area.

International law and principles governing territorial disputes

International law and principles play a crucial role in governing territorial disputes, such as the ongoing Guyana-Venezuela border dispute over the Esequibo oil-rich territory. This chapter delves into the intricate web of legal aspects, historical background, environmental impact, economic implications, geopolitical factors, social and cultural consequences, exploration and exploitation of oil resources, international mediation efforts, and the impact on regional stability and relations between Guyana and Venezuela. Additionally, it includes perspectives and opinions from local residents and stakeholders in the disputed area.

The Guyana-Venezuela border dispute has its roots in the colonial era when both countries were under British rule. Venezuela claims that the 1899 Arbitral Award, which settled the border between Guyana and Venezuela, is null and void. They argue that the territory awarded to Guyana, including the Esequibo region, rightfully belongs to them. Guyana, on the other hand, stands firmly by the validity of the Arbitral Award and asserts its sovereignty over the disputed area.

From a legal perspective, the principles of uti possidetis and the respect for existing borders are fundamental in resolving territorial disputes. These principles emphasize the importance of respecting the borders inherited from the colonial era, unless both parties agree to modify them. International law also provides mechanisms for dispute resolution, such as negotiation, mediation, and arbitration. Efforts have been made by both countries to resolve the dispute through various international platforms, including the United Nations and the International Court of Justice.

The environmental impact of the Esequibo oil-rich territory is a matter of concern. This region is home to diverse ecosystems, including rainforests and rivers. The exploration and exploitation of oil resources in the area pose risks of deforestation, pollution, and habitat destruction, which could have long-lasting effects on biodiversity and the livelihoods of local communities.

Economically, the Esequibo oil-rich territory holds significant potential for both Guyana and Venezuela. The discovery of oil reserves in recent years has sparked a race to tap into these resources. However, the border dispute has hindered the development of the oil industry in the region, leading to missed economic opportunities for both countries.

Geopolitical factors also influence the border dispute. The involvement of external actors, such as the United States and other regional powers, adds complexity to the issue. The dispute has implications for regional stability and relations between Guyana and Venezuela, affecting trade, cooperation, and regional integration efforts.

The social and cultural consequences of the dispute are felt by the affected communities living in the disputed area. These communities face uncertainties, displacement, and a sense of insecurity due to the unresolved border issue. The dispute has also strained relations between the peoples of Guyana and Venezuela, leading to tensions and mistrust.

Various perspectives and opinions from local residents and stakeholders in the disputed area shed light on the human dimension of the conflict. Their voices reflect the hopes, fears, and aspirations of those directly affected by the border dispute and offer insights into their experiences, concerns, and desires for a peaceful resolution.

In conclusion, the Guyana-Venezuela border dispute over the Esequibo oil-rich territory is a complex issue governed by international law and principles. It encompasses legal, historical, environmental, economic, geopolitical, social, and cultural dimensions. The dispute has significant implications for both countries and the region at large, impacting stability, cooperation, and the well-being of affected communities. Resolving this dispute requires a comprehensive understanding of these factors and a commitment to peaceful dialogue, mediation, and respect for international law.

Analysis of historical treaties and agreements

The Guyana-Venezuela border dispute and their claims over the Esequibo oil-rich territory have a deep-rooted historical background, marked by a series of treaties and agreements that have shaped the current state of affairs. Understanding the significance of these historical events is crucial in comprehending the complexities of the border dispute and its wide-ranging implications.

One of the pivotal treaties that laid the foundations for the border dispute is the 1899 Arbitral Award, also known as the Paris Award, which defined the borders between British Guiana (now Guyana) and Venezuela. However, Venezuela has consistently contested the validity of this award, arguing that it was biased and unjust. This disagreement has fueled the ongoing dispute over the Esequibo territory, which encompasses vast oil reserves.

From a legal standpoint, the border dispute is not merely a territorial disagreement but also raises important questions regarding international law and the interpretation of historical treaties. The legal aspects of the dispute involve examining the validity of the 1899 Arbitral Award and the subsequent agreements that have attempted to resolve the issue. Various legal arguments have been presented by both Guyana and Venezuela, making this a complex legal battleground.

The environmental impact of the Esequibo oil-rich territory is another significant aspect to consider. The exploration and exploitation of oil resources in the area have the potential to cause irreparable damage to the ecosystem and endanger the unique biodiversity found in the region. This raises concerns about the long-term sustainability of oil extraction in the disputed territory.

Moreover, the economic implications of the border dispute are immense. The Esequibo territory holds substantial oil reserves, which could significantly boost the economy of either Guyana or Venezuela. However, the dispute has hindered the development of the oil industry in the region, leading to missed economic opportunities for both countries.

Geopolitical factors also play a crucial role in shaping the border dispute. The strategic importance of the Esequibo territory and its oil reserves has attracted the attention of global powers, adding a complex layer to the already contentious issue. The involvement of external actors and their geopolitical interests further complicates the resolution of the dispute.

Furthermore, the social and cultural consequences of the border dispute on affected communities cannot be overlooked. The disputed area is home to indigenous communities whose lives and livelihoods are intertwined with the land. The uncertainty and tensions caused by the dispute have had a profound impact on these communities, leading to social and cultural disruptions.

International mediation efforts have been made to resolve the dispute, but so far, a definitive solution remains elusive. The impact of the border dispute on regional stability and relations between Guyana and Venezuela is significant, with potential implications for the wider Caribbean region.

Finally, it is crucial to consider the perspectives and opinions of local residents and stakeholders in the disputed area. Their voices provide invaluable insights into the human dimension of the border dispute and shed light on the lived experiences of those directly affected by the ongoing tensions.

In conclusion, the analysis of historical treaties and agreements is essential in understanding the Guyana-Venezuela border dispute and its wide-ranging implications. From the legal aspects to the environmental, economic, geopolitical, social, and cultural dimensions, this subchapter delves into the complexities of the dispute, providing a comprehensive overview for the public.

Examination of legal arguments from both sides

The Guyana-Venezuela border dispute over the Esequibo oil-rich territory has been a long-standing issue with complex legal arguments from both sides. This subchapter aims to provide an objective analysis of the legal aspects surrounding this contentious dispute.

From the Guyanese perspective, the legal argument is based on historical evidence. Guyana claims that the border between the two countries was established by the 1899 Arbitral Award, which clearly demarcated the boundaries. They emphasize that Venezuela accepted this decision for over half a century until the discovery of oil in the Esequibo region in the 1960s. Guyana argues that Venezuela's sudden claim to the territory is a result of economic interests rather than genuine legal concerns.

On the other hand, Venezuela argues that the 1899 Arbitral Award was invalid and that the border issue remains unresolved. They claim that the award was a product of coercion and that it failed to consider the rights of indigenous peoples in the region. Venezuela asserts that the Esequibo territory rightfully belongs to them and that they have historical evidence to support this claim.

International law plays a crucial role in examining the legal arguments from both sides. The United Nations Convention on the Law of the Sea (UNCLOS) is particularly relevant, as it governs the delimitation of maritime boundaries. While the dispute primarily concerns land territory, the potential for offshore oil exploration in the disputed area has made UNCLOS relevant to the discussion.

The legal arguments from both sides have been presented to various international bodies, including the International Court of Justice (ICJ). In 2018, the ICJ ruled that it had jurisdiction to hear the case, providing an opportunity for a legal resolution to the dispute. However, the final decision is yet to be reached.

It is important to note that legal arguments alone cannot fully address the complexities of the border dispute. Other factors, such as geopolitical interests, economic implications, and social consequences, also influence the dispute. Nevertheless, understanding the legal aspects is crucial in unraveling the intricacies of this long-standing issue.

In conclusion, the examination of legal arguments from both Guyana and Venezuela provides important insights into the nature of the border dispute over the Esequibo oil-rich territory. While historical evidence and international law play key roles in these arguments, a comprehensive understanding of the dispute requires consideration of other factors as well. By delving into the legal aspects, we can contribute to a balanced and informed discussion on this contentious issue.

Environmental impact of the Esequibo oil-rich territory

The Esequibo oil-rich territory, located in South America, has been at the center of a long-standing border dispute between Guyana and Venezuela. This subchapter aims to shed light on the environmental impact of this disputed region, an aspect often overlooked in discussions surrounding the border dispute.

The Esequibo oil-rich territory is known for its rich biodiversity and pristine ecosystems. It is home to numerous species of flora and fauna, some of which are endemic to the region. However, the ongoing territorial dispute has brought about significant environmental challenges. Both Guyana and Venezuela have sought to exploit the oil resources in the Esequibo, leading to increased deforestation, habitat destruction, and pollution.

The exploration and exploitation of oil resources in the Esequibo territory have resulted in the clearing of vast areas of forest, leading to the loss of critical habitat for numerous species. Additionally, the construction of infrastructure, such as roads and pipelines, has fragmented ecosystems and disrupted the natural flow of water, further exacerbating the environmental consequences.

Furthermore, the extraction and processing of oil in the region have resulted in the release of greenhouse gases and other pollutants, contributing to climate change and air pollution. This not only affects the local environment but also has broader implications for global climate patterns.

The environmental impact of the Esequibo oil-rich territory extends beyond the immediate ecological consequences. The destruction of natural habitats has also disrupted the livelihoods of local communities, many of whom rely on the land and its resources for sustenance. The loss of traditional livelihoods and cultural practices has had profound social and cultural consequences on these affected communities.

Efforts to resolve the border dispute and mitigate its environmental impact have been hindered by geopolitical factors and competing economic interests. International mediation efforts have been made, but a lasting resolution remains elusive. The lack of a clear resolution further exacerbates the environmental challenges faced by the Esequibo territory.

Perspectives and opinions from local residents and stakeholders in the disputed area are crucial in understanding the true impact of the border dispute. Their voices should be heard and considered in any discussion surrounding the future of the Esequibo oil-rich territory.

It is imperative that the environmental consequences of the Esequibo oil-rich territory are given due attention in any discourse surrounding the border dispute. A comprehensive and sustainable solution must be sought to protect the unique ecosystems and the communities that depend on them. Only through a holistic approach that considers the environmental, social, cultural, and economic implications can we hope to resolve this longstanding dispute and ensure a sustainable future for the region.

Biodiversity and ecological significance of the Esequibo region

The Esequibo region, located between Guyana and Venezuela, is a biodiversity hotspot of immense ecological significance. This subchapter will delve into the rich natural resources and unique ecosystems found in this disputed territory, highlighting their importance and the need for their preservation.

The Esequibo region is characterized by its diverse landscapes, ranging from pristine rainforests to expansive savannahs. It is home to a vast array of plant and animal species, many of which are endemic to the region. The dense forests provide habitat for numerous endangered species, including jaguars, giant anteaters, and the elusive harpy eagle. The rivers and wetlands support a diverse range of aquatic life, including several species of rare fish and turtles.

The ecological significance of the Esequibo region extends beyond its biodiversity. The forests act as a carbon sink, absorbing vast amounts of carbon dioxide and playing a crucial role in mitigating climate change. They also regulate local and regional climate patterns, maintaining a stable environment for both human and animal communities. The region's rivers are a vital source of freshwater, providing sustenance and livelihoods for local communities.

However, the ongoing border dispute between Guyana and Venezuela poses a significant threat to the ecological integrity of the Esequibo region. Exploration and exploitation of oil resources in this territory could lead to deforestation, pollution, and habitat fragmentation. These activities could have severe consequences for both local communities and the unique ecosystems that rely on the region's pristine environment.

Efforts to resolve the border dispute have included international mediation, but progress has been slow. The lack of a definitive resolution has left the Esequibo region vulnerable to potential environmental degradation and destruction. It is crucial for both Guyana and Venezuela, as well as the international community, to recognize the ecological significance of this area and work towards its preservation.

Local residents and stakeholders in the disputed area have expressed their concerns about the potential environmental impacts of the dispute. They emphasize the need for sustainable development practices that prioritize the protection of the region's biodiversity and ecosystems. Their perspectives and opinions should be taken into account in any future discussions and decision-making processes related to the Esequibo region.

In conclusion, the Esequibo region is a biodiverse and ecologically significant area, deserving of protection and preservation. The ongoing border dispute between Guyana and Venezuela poses a threat to its unique ecosystems and the communities that depend on them. It is crucial for all stakeholders, including the public, to understand the environmental implications of this dispute and advocate for sustainable practices that prioritize the region's biodiversity and ecological integrity.

Potential risks and challenges of oil exploration and extraction

The exploration and extraction of oil resources in the Esequibo territory, amidst the ongoing Guyana-Venezuela border dispute, present numerous risks and challenges that must be carefully considered. These risks and challenges encompass various aspects, including environmental, economic, geopolitical, and social consequences.

One of the primary concerns is the potential environmental impact of oil exploration and extraction in the Esequibo oil-rich territory. Oil drilling activities can lead to habitat destruction, pollution of water bodies, and the release of greenhouse gases, contributing to climate change. This could have severe implications for the unique and fragile ecosystems in the region, including the rich biodiversity found in the rainforests and rivers.

Economically, the border dispute and its implications for oil exploration pose challenges for both Guyana and Venezuela. Uncertainty surrounding ownership and control of the Esequibo territory hampers investment and leaves potential investors wary of committing resources. Additionally, the legal and financial complexities surrounding the border dispute can deter international companies from participating in oil exploration and extraction activities in the region.

Geopolitically, the border dispute and the potential exploitation of oil resources have implications for regional stability and relations between Guyana and Venezuela. The dispute has already strained diplomatic relations, and any escalation could have wider regional consequences. It is crucial to carefully manage the geopolitical factors involved to prevent further tensions and potential conflicts.

The social and cultural consequences of the border dispute on affected communities cannot be overlooked. The disputed area is home to indigenous communities and other local residents who have lived there for generations. The exploration and extraction activities could lead to displacement, cultural erosion, and social unrest, impacting the lives and livelihoods of these communities.

Furthermore, the border dispute has attracted international attention, prompting various mediation efforts to resolve the issue. These efforts, although well-intentioned, have yet to yield a definitive solution. The involvement of international actors in the dispute adds another layer of complexity and uncertainty to the situation.

To gain a comprehensive understanding of the risks and challenges, it is essential to consider the perspectives and opinions of local residents and stakeholders in the disputed area. Their voices can shed light on the potential impacts and provide valuable insights into the best path forward.

In conclusion, the potential risks and challenges associated with oil exploration and extraction in the Esequibo oil-rich territory are multifaceted. They encompass environmental, economic, geopolitical, and social dimensions. It is crucial for all stakeholders involved to carefully navigate these challenges and work towards a resolution that prioritizes sustainable development, environmental conservation, and the well-being of affected communities.

Sustainable development and environmental considerations

Sustainable development and environmental considerations play a crucial role in the Guyana-Venezuela border dispute and their claims over the Esequibo oil-rich territory. This subchapter delves into the various aspects of sustainable development and the environmental implications of this long-standing dispute.

Historically, the Guyana-Venezuela border dispute has its roots in the colonial era when conflicting territorial claims were made by both countries. This dispute has significant legal ramifications, as both nations have presented their cases based on historical documents and international law. However, the environmental impact of the Esequibo oil-rich territory is an equally important concern.

The exploration and exploitation of oil resources in the Esequibo territory have raised environmental concerns among experts and environmentalists. The extraction of oil not only leads to deforestation and habitat destruction but also contributes to greenhouse gas emissions and climate change. The delicate balance of ecosystems in the region is at stake, posing a threat to unique flora and fauna found in this biodiverse area.

Moreover, the economic implications of the border dispute are closely intertwined with the environmental concerns. The Esequibo territory holds vast reserves of oil, making it a highly coveted region for both countries. However, the potential economic benefits must be considered in tandem with sustainable development practices to ensure the long-term well-being of the region and its communities.

Geopolitical factors also influence the border dispute, as neighboring countries and international players have vested interests in the outcome. The dispute has strained regional stability and relations between Guyana and Venezuela, affecting the social and cultural fabric of the affected communities. Local residents and stakeholders have unique perspectives and opinions on the matter, which should be taken into account during any resolution process.

International mediation efforts have been made to resolve the border dispute, with various organizations and countries involved in facilitating negotiations between Guyana and Venezuela. These mediation efforts should consider not only the political and legal aspects but also the environmental and sustainable development concerns.

In conclusion, sustainable development and environmental considerations are crucial elements in the Guyana-Venezuela border dispute and their claims over the Esequibo oil-rich territory. The exploration and exploitation of oil resources must be approached with caution to mitigate the environmental impact and ensure the well-being of the region's ecosystems and communities. International mediation efforts should take into account the perspectives and opinions of local residents and stakeholders, as their livelihoods and cultural heritage are at stake. By addressing these concerns, a more balanced and sustainable resolution to the border dispute can be achieved, fostering regional stability and cooperation.

Economic implications of the Guyana-Venezuela border dispute

The Guyana-Venezuela border dispute over the Esequibo oil-rich territory has significant economic implications for both countries and the wider region. The disputed area is believed to contain vast oil and natural gas reserves, making it a highly valuable economic asset.

For Guyana, the potential exploitation of oil resources in the Esequibo territory holds the promise of transforming the country's economy. With the discovery of major offshore oil fields, Guyana has the potential to become a major oil-producing nation. However, the border dispute with Venezuela has created uncertainty and hindered investment in the sector. Oil companies are cautious about investing in Guyana's oil industry due to the risk of legal disputes and potential disruptions to operations. This has slowed down the development of the sector and delayed the economic benefits that could be derived from oil production.

On the other hand, Venezuela's stake in the border dispute is motivated by its economic challenges. The country is facing a severe economic crisis characterized by hyperinflation, shortages of basic goods, and a declining oil industry. The disputed Esequibo territory represents an opportunity for Venezuela to access new oil reserves and potentially revive its struggling economy. However, the border dispute has made it difficult for Venezuela to attract the necessary international investment and expertise to develop these resources.

The economic implications of the border dispute extend beyond the two countries directly involved. The potential oil wealth in the Esequibo territory has attracted the attention of major global powers, including the United States, China, and Russia. These countries have a vested interest in securing access to the resources and are closely monitoring the border dispute. Their involvement adds a geopolitical dimension to the conflict, further complicating its resolution.

The ongoing border dispute also affects regional stability and relations between Guyana and Venezuela. The two countries have a history of strained diplomatic ties, and the dispute has exacerbated tensions. It has led to military deployments along the border, increased rhetoric, and occasional incidents of aggression. This has created an environment of uncertainty and instability, deterring investment and economic cooperation between the two neighbors.

In conclusion, the economic implications of the Guyana-Venezuela border dispute are far-reaching. The potential exploitation of oil resources in the Esequibo territory holds significant economic benefits for both countries. However, the dispute has created uncertainty, hindered investment, and strained regional relations. Resolving the border dispute is crucial for unlocking the economic potential of the region and ensuring the long-term stability and prosperity of both Guyana and Venezuela.

Oil reserves and their potential economic benefits

The Esequibo region, located at the border between Guyana and Venezuela, is known for its vast oil reserves. These oil reserves have the potential to bring significant economic benefits to both countries. In this subchapter, we will explore the economic implications of the Guyana-Venezuela border dispute and the opportunities that lie within the Esequibo oil-rich territory.

The Esequibo region is estimated to hold significant oil reserves, which could potentially transform the economies of both Guyana and Venezuela. Oil exploration and exploitation in this area could lead to increased employment opportunities, foreign direct investment, and government revenue. Furthermore, the revenue generated from oil production could be used to fund infrastructure development, education, and healthcare, benefiting the local population.

However, the border dispute between Guyana and Venezuela has hindered the exploration and exploitation of these oil resources. The legal aspects of the dispute have created uncertainty for investors and have prevented the full potential of the Esequibo oil-rich territory from being realized. International mediation efforts have been made to resolve the dispute, but a final resolution is yet to be reached.

The geopolitical factors influencing the border dispute also play a significant role in the economic implications. Both Guyana and Venezuela have sought support from regional and international allies, further complicating the situation. This has created instability in the region and strained relations between the two countries, negatively impacting trade and cooperation.

Moreover, the environmental impact of oil production in the Esequibo region must also be considered. Proper environmental regulations and safeguards need to be in place to prevent any negative consequences on the fragile ecosystem. The exploitation of oil resources should be done in a sustainable manner to ensure the long-term well-being of the region.

The social and cultural consequences of the dispute on affected communities cannot be ignored. The uncertainty and tension created by the border dispute have caused anxiety and fear among the local population. Their livelihoods and cultural heritage have been affected, as the dispute has disrupted their way of life and limited their access to resources.

To gain a comprehensive understanding of the situation, it is essential to consider the perspectives and opinions of local residents and stakeholders in the disputed area. Their voices should be heard in any decision-making process to ensure that their interests are taken into account.

In conclusion, the Esequibo oil-rich territory holds great potential for economic benefits for both Guyana and Venezuela. However, the border dispute and its legal, environmental, geopolitical, and social implications have hindered the exploration and exploitation of these resources. A peaceful resolution to the dispute, along with sustainable practices and the involvement of local stakeholders, is crucial to unlocking the economic potential of the Esequibo region.

Impact on investment and economic growth in Guyana

The Guyana-Venezuela border dispute and their claims over the Esequibo oil-rich territory have had significant implications for investment and economic growth in Guyana. This subchapter explores the various aspects of this impact.

Firstly, the historical background of the border dispute has created uncertainty and instability, deterring potential investors from committing their resources to Guyana. The disputed territory is known to be rich in oil reserves, making it an attractive prospect for exploration and exploitation. However, the ongoing dispute has made investors wary of the potential risks and complications associated with investing in this region. As a result, Guyana has struggled to attract the necessary capital and expertise to fully tap into its oil resources, hampering its economic growth.

Furthermore, the legal aspects of the border dispute have raised concerns about the security of property rights and contracts in Guyana. Investors require a stable legal framework that guarantees the protection of their investments. However, the dispute has cast doubt on the enforceability of contracts and property rights in the disputed area, creating a challenging environment for investment.

The environmental impact of the Esequibo oil-rich territory is another important consideration. Oil exploration and extraction can have significant environmental consequences, including pollution, deforestation, and habitat destruction. The dispute has hindered the establishment of robust environmental regulations and oversight, increasing the risk of environmental damage. This has further dampened investor confidence and limited economic growth opportunities in the region.

Geopolitical factors have also influenced the border dispute and, consequently, investment and economic growth in Guyana. Venezuela's political instability and its economic crisis have contributed to the escalation of the dispute. The geopolitical tensions have created a volatile environment, discouraging investment and hindering economic development.

The social and cultural consequences of the dispute on affected communities cannot be overlooked. The uncertainty and tension surrounding the border dispute have disrupted the lives of people living in the disputed area. Local communities have been displaced, livelihoods have been affected, and social cohesion has been undermined. These social and cultural consequences have further compounded the economic challenges faced by the affected communities.

Efforts to resolve the border dispute through international mediation have had limited success. The lack of a definitive resolution has meant that the investment climate remains uncertain, hindering economic growth in Guyana.

In conclusion, the Guyana-Venezuela border dispute and their claims over the Esequibo oil-rich territory have had a significant impact on investment and economic growth in Guyana. The historical, legal, environmental, geopolitical, and social factors associated with the dispute have created an uncertain and challenging investment climate.

Resolving the dispute and providing a stable legal and regulatory framework will be crucial for attracting investment and fostering economic growth in Guyana.

Economic consequences for Venezuela and regional trade

The Guyana-Venezuela border dispute and their claims over the Esequibo oil-rich territory have had significant economic implications for both Venezuela and the region as a whole. The disputed territory is believed to have vast oil reserves, which has attracted the attention of major international oil companies. However, due to the ongoing border dispute, exploration and exploitation of these resources have been severely hindered.

Venezuela, once a major oil-producing nation, has seen its economy suffer greatly in recent years. The decline in oil prices coupled with mismanagement and corruption has led to hyperinflation, shortages of basic goods, and a deep economic crisis. The disputed Esequibo territory could have been a potential lifeline for Venezuela, providing much-needed revenue and boosting its struggling economy. However, the border dispute has prevented Venezuela from fully capitalizing on these resources.

Furthermore, the border dispute has also affected regional trade. Guyana, with its stable political climate and growing oil industry, has become an attractive destination for foreign investment. However, the uncertainty surrounding the border dispute has deterred some potential investors who fear the risk of future conflicts and legal disputes. This has limited the economic growth potential of Guyana and hindered the development of regional trade.

The geopolitical factors influencing the border dispute have also had economic consequences. Venezuela, under the leadership of President Nicolás Maduro, has sought to maintain control over the disputed territory, viewing it as a matter of national sovereignty. This has strained relations with neighboring countries, including Guyana, and led to tensions within the region. The resulting instability has discouraged foreign investment and hindered regional cooperation in trade and development initiatives.

The social and cultural consequences of the dispute on affected communities cannot be overlooked either. The disputed area is home to indigenous communities who have been greatly affected by the border dispute. Their traditional way of life, which relies heavily on fishing and farming, has been disrupted, leading to social and economic dislocation. The uncertainty surrounding land ownership and resource rights has further exacerbated the situation, leaving these communities vulnerable and marginalized.

Efforts to resolve the border dispute through international mediation have been ongoing for years. The United Nations and other international organizations have been involved in facilitating talks between Guyana and Venezuela. However, a resolution has yet to be reached, prolonging the economic consequences for both countries and the region as a whole.

Perspectives and opinions from local residents and stakeholders in the disputed area vary. Some argue for a swift resolution to the dispute, highlighting the economic benefits that could be gained. Others emphasize the importance of preserving the rights and interests of indigenous communities and ensuring sustainable development in the region.

In conclusion, the Guyana-Venezuela border dispute and their claims over the Esequibo oil-rich territory have had far-reaching economic consequences for Venezuela and regional trade. The dispute has hindered the exploration and exploitation of valuable oil resources, leading to economic stagnation for Venezuela and limiting the growth potential of Guyana. The geopolitical factors, social and cultural consequences, and ongoing international mediation efforts further compound the economic implications of the dispute. The perspectives and opinions of local residents and stakeholders highlight the complexity of the issue and the need for a balanced and sustainable resolution.

Geopolitical factors influencing the border dispute

Geopolitical factors play a crucial role in influencing the long-standing border dispute between Guyana and Venezuela over the Esequibo oil-rich territory. These factors encompass a range of political, economic, and strategic considerations that contribute to the complexity and endurance of the dispute.

One significant geopolitical factor is the strategic importance of the Esequibo territory due to its vast oil resources. The discovery of oil reserves in this disputed area has intensified the dispute and increased its geopolitical significance. Both Guyana and Venezuela recognize the potential economic benefits that the oil-rich territory could bring, including revenue generation, foreign investment, and energy security. The pursuit of these economic gains has further entrenched their respective claims over the region.

Moreover, the broader geopolitical dynamics of the region also influence the border dispute. Venezuela's historical role as a regional power and its aspirations for regional hegemony have implications for the territorial dispute. Venezuela's internal political and economic challenges have led the government to adopt a more assertive and nationalist stance on the border issue, using it as a rallying point to divert attention from internal issues and bolster domestic support.

Additionally, the involvement of external actors in the dispute has geopolitical implications. The United States, as a global power with interests in the region, has been supportive of Guyana's claims and has taken steps to strengthen its relationship with the country. This support is largely motivated by the desire to counterbalance Venezuela's influence and assertiveness in the region. Other countries, such as Russia and China, also have economic and strategic interests in the disputed area, making the dispute a focal point for their geopolitical calculations.

Furthermore, the border dispute has implications for regional stability and relations between Guyana and Venezuela. The tension and uncertainty surrounding the dispute have the potential to destabilize the region, with the possibility of military escalation or other conflicts. The dispute also hampers cooperation and integration efforts within the Caribbean Community (CARICOM), as member states are divided in their support for either Guyana or Venezuela.

In conclusion, the geopolitical factors influencing the border dispute between Guyana and Venezuela are multifaceted and have far-reaching consequences. The strategic importance of the Esequibo oil-rich territory, the broader regional dynamics, the involvement of external actors, and the impact on regional stability all contribute to the complexity and endurance of the dispute. Understanding these factors is crucial for comprehending the ongoing challenges and potential resolutions to the Guyana-Venezuela border dispute.

Influence of major powers and regional dynamics

The Guyana-Venezuela border dispute over the Esequibo oil-rich territory is not only a matter between two neighboring countries but also a complex issue that involves major powers and regional dynamics. The influence of these powers and regional dynamics has played a significant role in shaping the outcome of the dispute and its impact on the affected communities.

One of the major powers that have influenced the border dispute is the United States. As a global superpower with interests in the region, the United States has been closely monitoring the situation and has shown support for Guyana in its territorial claims. This support has been seen through various diplomatic efforts and economic aid to strengthen Guyana's position. The United States' involvement has added a geopolitical dimension to the dispute, as it strives to maintain its influence in the region and counterbalance the influence of other major powers.

Another major power that has influenced the dispute is China. With its growing economic presence in Latin America, China has become an important player in the region. Both Guyana and Venezuela have sought Chinese investments and support, which has further complicated the dispute. China's interests in the Esequibo oil-rich territory have led to increased competition with other major powers, particularly the United States. This competition has exacerbated tensions and made resolution more challenging.

Regional dynamics have also played a significant role in the border dispute. The Caribbean Community (CARICOM) has been actively involved in mediating the conflict and encouraging both parties to find a peaceful solution. CARICOM's efforts have been crucial in maintaining regional stability and preventing the dispute from escalating into a larger conflict. Additionally, other neighboring countries, such as Brazil and Colombia, have been affected by the dispute due to their proximity to the Esequibo territory. These countries have had to navigate their own relationships with Guyana and Venezuela, further complicating the regional dynamics.

The influence of major powers and regional dynamics on the Guyana-Venezuela border dispute cannot be underestimated. These factors have shaped the strategies and positions of the involved parties, as well as the overall trajectory of the dispute. Furthermore, they have had profound implications for the affected communities, both socially and economically. As the dispute continues, it is essential to consider the influence of these powers and dynamics in order to understand the complexities and potential outcomes of the ongoing conflict.

Geopolitical interests and alliances in the South American region

The South American region has long been a hotbed of geopolitical tensions and interests, and the Guyana-Venezuela border dispute over the Esequibo Oil-Rich Territory is no exception. This subchapter explores the various factors that have shaped the dispute and its broader implications on regional stability and relations between Guyana and Venezuela.

Historically, the border dispute dates back to the colonial era when Spain and Britain claimed overlapping territories. Despite the subsequent independence of both countries, the issue remained unresolved, with Venezuela asserting its claim over the Esequibo region. This dispute has not only had legal implications but has also impacted the social and cultural fabric of the affected communities.

One of the key drivers of the border dispute is the economic potential of the Esequibo territory. With vast oil resources believed to be present in the region, both Guyana and Venezuela have significant economic interests at stake. The exploration and exploitation of these oil resources have the potential to transform the economies of both countries, attracting international attention and investment.

However, the dispute has not been limited to economic considerations alone. Geopolitical factors have also played a crucial role. The strategic location of the disputed area has drawn the attention of other regional and global powers. Some countries, such as the United States, have supported Guyana, while others, like Russia and China, have aligned themselves with Venezuela. These alliances have added complexity to the already tense situation, with geopolitical interests further fueling the dispute.

International mediation efforts have been ongoing for years, with various entities, including the United Nations, attempting to find a resolution. However, progress has been slow, and the dispute continues to impact regional stability. The uncertainty surrounding the border has strained relations between Guyana and Venezuela, leading to diplomatic tensions and occasional military posturing.

Local residents and stakeholders in the disputed area have been greatly affected by the ongoing dispute. The social and cultural consequences have been significant, with communities living in a state of uncertainty and insecurity. Perspectives and opinions from these individuals provide valuable insights into the human impact of the dispute and highlight the need for a timely resolution.

In conclusion, the Guyana-Venezuela border dispute over the Esequibo Oil-Rich Territory is a complex issue shaped by geopolitical interests, economic considerations, legal aspects, and environmental impacts. Its resolution is crucial not only for the affected countries but also for regional stability. Efforts must be made to address the concerns of local residents and stakeholders and find a mutually acceptable solution that respects the rights and aspirations of all parties involved.

Security concerns and the militarization of the border

The Guyana-Venezuela border dispute over the Esequibo oil-rich territory has not only stirred up tensions between the two nations but has also raised significant security concerns, leading to the militarization of the border. This subchapter explores the various dimensions of these security concerns and their implications for both nations and the wider region.

Historically, the disputed border area has been subject to incursions and clashes between Guyanese and Venezuelan military forces. Both countries have deployed troops to the region, creating an atmosphere of hostility and mistrust. The militarization of the border has not only heightened tensions but has also increased the risk of armed conflict between the two nations.

The presence of military forces in the disputed area also has a direct impact on the affected communities. Local residents live under constant fear and insecurity due to the militarization of their surroundings. Their daily lives are disrupted, and their livelihoods are at risk. The militarization of the border has not only caused physical and psychological harm to these communities but has also led to the displacement of people from their homes.

Furthermore, the militarization of the border has significant implications for regional stability and relations between Guyana and Venezuela. The increased military presence has strained diplomatic ties and hindered efforts for peaceful resolution. It has also attracted the attention of other regional and international actors, potentially exacerbating the conflict and complicating mediation efforts.

The environmental impact of the Esequibo oil-rich territory adds another layer of concern. The presence of military forces in the region poses a threat to the fragile ecosystem, including the rich biodiversity and pristine natural resources. The risk of oil spills or other forms of environmental degradation looms large, further exacerbating the already fragile ecological balance.

In addition to environmental concerns, the militarization of the border has severe economic implications. The escalating tensions and insecurity deter foreign investment and economic development in the disputed area. Exploitation of the oil resources in the Esequibo territory is put on hold, limiting the potential for economic growth and depriving both nations of significant revenue.

To address these security concerns, international mediation efforts have been ongoing. However, the militarization of the border poses a formidable challenge to achieving a peaceful resolution. The perspectives and opinions of local residents and stakeholders in the disputed area must also be taken into account to ensure a comprehensive understanding of the security concerns and potential solutions.

In conclusion, the security concerns stemming from the Guyana-Venezuela border dispute and the subsequent militarization of the border have far-reaching implications for both nations and the wider region. The presence of military forces disrupts the lives of local communities, threatens the environment, hampers economic development, and strains regional stability. Efforts must be made to de-escalate tensions, promote peaceful resolution, and prioritize the safety and well-being of the affected communities.

Social and cultural consequences of the dispute on affected communities

The Guyana-Venezuela border dispute over the Esequibo oil-rich territory has far-reaching social and cultural consequences for the affected communities. This contentious issue has caused tension, division, and uncertainty among the people living in the disputed area, impacting their daily lives and future prospects.

One of the most significant social consequences is the disruption of communal ties and relationships between neighboring communities. The border dispute has created a sense of animosity and suspicion among residents who once lived harmoniously. Families and friends find themselves on opposing sides, torn apart by the disagreement. This has led to a breakdown in social cohesion, as people are forced to choose between their national allegiances and their personal connections.

Cultural identity is another aspect deeply affected by the border dispute. The disputed region is home to diverse indigenous communities, each with its unique cultural heritage. The uncertainty surrounding the territory's ownership has resulted in a loss of cultural confidence and pride. Communities are fearful of losing their ancestral lands and traditions, leading to a sense of cultural erasure and displacement.

Moreover, the dispute has also had an adverse impact on education and healthcare in the affected communities. The lack of clarity and ongoing tensions have deterred investments in these vital sectors, leaving residents with limited access to quality education and healthcare facilities. The resulting socio-economic disparity further exacerbates the marginalization of these communities.

Furthermore, the border dispute has hindered economic development in the region. Investors are reluctant to commit resources due to the uncertain legal and territorial status. This has resulted in limited job opportunities and economic growth, forcing many residents to seek livelihoods elsewhere. As a result, the affected communities face both economic hardships and the loss of their traditional ways of life.

The social and cultural consequences of the Guyana-Venezuela border dispute are profound and enduring. They go beyond the legal and geopolitical aspects of the issue. It is imperative for governments, international organizations, and stakeholders to recognize and address these consequences. Only through dialogue, understanding, and inclusive policies can the affected communities begin to heal and rebuild their lives in the face of this ongoing dispute.

Displacement and migration patterns

The Guyana-Venezuela border dispute over the Esequibo oil-rich territory has had profound consequences on the lives of the people living in the disputed area. Displacement and migration patterns have been a significant result of this long-standing conflict, impacting both the local communities and the wider region.

Historically, the dispute has caused waves of migration as people sought safety and stability away from the conflict zone. Many have been forced to abandon their homes and livelihoods, leaving behind their ancestral lands due to the uncertainty and tensions surrounding the border dispute. This has led to a significant disruption in the lives of those affected, as they are forced to rebuild their lives in unfamiliar territories.

The displacement and migration patterns have not only affected individuals and families but also entire communities. The social fabric of these communities has been torn apart, as families and friends are separated, and traditional cultural practices are disrupted. The loss of connection to ancestral lands has had a profound impact on the cultural identity and heritage of these communities, leading to a sense of loss and displacement.

Furthermore, the economic implications of the border dispute have also contributed to migration patterns. The Esequibo oil-rich territory is believed to hold vast reserves of oil and natural resources, making it an attractive prospect for economic development. As a result, there has been an influx of people, both from within Guyana and Venezuela and from other regions, seeking economic opportunities in the disputed area. This has further complicated the situation, as it has led to an increase in population and competition for resources, exacerbating tensions between the two countries.

The environmental impact of the Esequibo oil-rich territory has also played a role in displacement and migration patterns. The exploration and exploitation of oil resources in the area have led to environmental degradation and pollution, forcing communities to abandon their homes and seek refuge elsewhere. The loss of access to clean water, fertile land, and natural resources has contributed to the displacement of communities and further fueled migration patterns.

In conclusion, the Guyana-Venezuela border dispute over the Esequibo oil-rich territory has had far-reaching consequences on displacement and migration patterns. The uncertainty and tensions surrounding the conflict have forced people to leave their homes, leading to the disruption of communities and the loss of cultural identity. The economic implications and environmental impact of the dispute have further contributed to migration patterns in the region. It is crucial to consider the human cost of this long-standing conflict and work towards finding a peaceful resolution that respects the rights and well-being of the affected communities.

Cultural heritage and identity preservation

Cultural heritage and identity preservation play a significant role in the ongoing Guyana-Venezuela border dispute and their claims over the Esequibo oil-rich territory. This subchapter aims to explore the impact of the dispute on the preservation of cultural heritage and the identity of the affected communities.

The Guyana-Venezuela border dispute has a long historical background, dating back to the colonial era. The contested Esequibo territory holds immense cultural significance for both countries. It is home to indigenous communities, such as the Wapishana, Macushi, and Akawaio, who have inhabited the region for centuries. These communities have developed unique cultural practices, traditions, and languages that are deeply intertwined with the territory.

The legal aspects of the border dispute have further complicated the preservation of cultural heritage. The lack of a definitive border demarcation has led to uncertainty and insecurity among the affected communities. This has resulted in the erosion and loss of cultural practices and traditions, as people are forced to adapt to changing circumstances and external pressures.

The environmental impact of the Esequibo oil-rich territory has also posed challenges to cultural heritage preservation. The exploration and exploitation of oil resources have led to deforestation, pollution, and the destruction of sacred sites. These activities not only harm the environment but also threaten the cultural practices and spiritual connections of the indigenous communities.

The economic implications of the border dispute have further exacerbated the challenges faced by the affected communities. The dispute has hindered economic development, as investment and tourism opportunities in the Esequibo territory are put on hold. This has resulted in limited resources for cultural preservation activities and the struggle to maintain cultural institutions and heritage sites.

Geopolitical factors have also influenced the border dispute and its impact on cultural heritage. The involvement of external actors and their vested interests often overshadow the voices and needs of the local residents and stakeholders. This further marginalizes the cultural identity of the affected communities and hampers their ability to preserve and transmit their heritage to future generations.

International mediation efforts have been made to resolve the border dispute, but their effectiveness remains uncertain. The impact of the dispute on regional stability and relations between Guyana and Venezuela is also a significant concern. The ongoing tensions and uncertainty regarding the territorial claims have created an atmosphere of anxiety and fear among the affected communities, further endangering the preservation of their cultural heritage.

In conclusion, the Guyana-Venezuela border dispute and their claims over the Esequibo oil-rich territory have had profound social and cultural consequences on the affected communities. The erosion of cultural practices, loss of sacred sites, and limited resources for preservation activities have threatened the cultural heritage and identity of the indigenous communities. It is essential for international organizations and stakeholders to recognize and address these challenges to ensure the preservation and transmission of cultural heritage for future generations.

Social cohesion and community relations in the disputed area

Social cohesion and community relations are crucial aspects to consider when examining the disputed area between Guyana and Venezuela, particularly the Esequibo oil-rich territory. This subchapter aims to shed light on the impact of the border dispute on social dynamics and community relations in the affected area.

The border dispute between Guyana and Venezuela has a long and complex historical background. Both countries have been claiming sovereignty over the Esequibo territory for centuries, leading to tensions and occasional outbreaks of violence. This dispute has had significant social and cultural consequences on the affected communities.

The ongoing territorial disagreement has created a sense of uncertainty and instability among the residents of the disputed area. Everyday life has been disrupted, as the residents have to navigate through the complexities of living in a contested territory. This has resulted in heightened social tensions and divisions within communities, as individuals align themselves with either the Guyanese or Venezuelan side.

The exploration and exploitation of oil resources in the Esequibo territory have exacerbated these social divisions. The prospect of oil wealth has attracted multinational companies and investment, leading to an influx of outsiders into the area. This has caused tensions between the local communities and the newcomers, as resources become scarce and competition for jobs and opportunities intensifies.

The border dispute has also had an impact on regional stability and relations between Guyana and Venezuela. The two countries have engaged in diplomatic spats and political maneuvering, which has strained their diplomatic ties. This has trickled down to the local level, where residents have experienced a deterioration in cross-border exchanges and interactions.

International mediation efforts have been made to resolve the border dispute, but progress has been slow. The lack of a definitive resolution has perpetuated the social and cultural consequences on the affected communities. Local residents and stakeholders in the disputed area have voiced their perspectives and opinions, with some advocating for a peaceful resolution, while others hold onto their nationalistic sentiments.

In conclusion, the social cohesion and community relations in the disputed area between Guyana and Venezuela have been greatly affected by the ongoing border dispute. The uncertainty and instability created by the territorial disagreement have led to social tensions, divisions, and strained relations between the affected communities. The exploration and exploitation of oil resources have further exacerbated these issues. It is crucial to consider the social and cultural consequences when examining the complexities of the Guyana-Venezuela border dispute and its impact on the Esequibo oil-rich territory.

Exploration and exploitation of oil resources in the Esequibo territory

The Esequibo territory, a region rich in oil resources, has been at the center of a longstanding border dispute between Guyana and Venezuela. This subchapter aims to shed light on the exploration and exploitation of oil resources in this disputed area and its implications for both countries and the international community.

The Esequibo territory, located in the northeastern part of South America, has been claimed by both Guyana and Venezuela for centuries. This dispute has hindered the development and utilization of the vast oil resources present in the region. The exploration and exploitation of these resources hold immense economic potential for both countries, attracting the attention of various stakeholders and international players.

Despite the ongoing border dispute, oil companies have shown significant interest in the Esequibo territory. The potential reserves of oil and natural gas in the region have been estimated to be substantial, making it a highly attractive investment opportunity. However, the disputed status of the area has made oil exploration and extraction challenging, as companies face legal and geopolitical uncertainties.

The environmental impact of oil exploration and exploitation in the Esequibo territory cannot be overlooked. The delicate ecosystems, including rainforests and rivers, are at risk of irreversible damage due to oil spills, deforestation, and pollution. Such environmental consequences pose a threat not only to the local communities but also to the broader region's biodiversity and ecosystem balance.

Furthermore, the border dispute has had significant social and cultural consequences for the affected communities. The uncertainty surrounding land ownership has led to displacement, conflicts, and a sense of insecurity among residents. The cultural heritage and traditional way of life of these communities are also at risk of being eroded.

Efforts have been made by international mediators to resolve the border dispute between Guyana and Venezuela. However, the complex geopolitical factors and vested interests involved have hampered progress. The resolution of this dispute holds importance not only for the two countries involved but also for regional stability and international relations.

In conclusion, the exploration and exploitation of oil resources in the Esequibo territory present both opportunities and challenges for Guyana, Venezuela, and the international community. The environmental, economic, and social implications of this dispute are far-reaching and require careful consideration. International mediation and dialogue are crucial in finding a resolution that safeguards the interests of all stakeholders, including the affected communities and the environment. Only through a peaceful resolution can the potential benefits of the Esequibo territory be realized while minimizing its negative impacts.

Current and planned oil projects in the Esequibo region

The Esequibo region, a disputed territory between Guyana and Venezuela, is known for its vast oil-rich reserves. This subchapter focuses on the current and planned oil projects in this region and their implications for various stakeholders.

Over the past few years, the Esequibo region has witnessed a surge in oil exploration and exploitation activities. International oil companies have shown great interest in tapping into the potential of this area, despite the ongoing border dispute. Guyana, with the support of international partners, has been actively promoting investment in the region to bolster its economy.

One of the major oil projects in the Esequibo region is the Liza Field, discovered by ExxonMobil in 2015. This offshore field is estimated to hold billions of barrels of oil reserves. ExxonMobil, along with its partners, has been developing the Liza Phase 1 and 2 projects, which are expected to contribute significantly to Guyana's oil production capacity.

In addition to ExxonMobil, other international oil companies such as Hess Corporation and CNOOC have also secured exploration licenses in the Esequibo region. These companies are conducting seismic surveys and drilling operations to identify potential oil reservoirs.

However, the planned and ongoing oil projects in the Esequibo region have raised concerns regarding their environmental impact. The fragile ecosystems, including pristine rainforests and diverse wildlife habitats, are at risk due to potential oil spills and deforestation associated with oil exploration and extraction.

Moreover, the border dispute between Guyana and Venezuela adds another layer of complexity to these projects. Venezuela claims sovereignty over the Esequibo region, challenging the legitimacy of oil exploration activities conducted by foreign companies in the area. This dispute has led to tensions between the two neighboring countries and has the potential to escalate if not resolved peacefully.

International mediation efforts have been made to resolve the border dispute, but a final resolution remains elusive. The uncertainty surrounding the ownership of the Esequibo region has implications for regional stability and relations between Guyana and Venezuela.

The social and cultural consequences of this dispute on the affected communities cannot be overlooked. The people living in the disputed area are caught in the crossfire, facing uncertainty and insecurity. Their perspectives and opinions must be taken into account when considering the future of the Esequibo region.

In conclusion, the current and planned oil projects in the Esequibo region hold significant economic implications for Guyana and attract international investment. However, the environmental, geopolitical, and social consequences of these projects, combined with the ongoing border dispute, raise important questions that must be addressed for the sustainable development of the region.

Technological advancements and extraction techniques

Technological advancements and extraction techniques have played a significant role in shaping the ongoing border dispute between Guyana and Venezuela over the Esequibo oil-rich territory. This subchapter will delve into the various ways in which technology has impacted the exploration and exploitation of oil resources in this disputed area.

Over the years, advancements in seismic imaging technology have revolutionized the oil industry, allowing companies to accurately map subsurface structures and identify potential oil reserves. This technology has been crucial in the Esequibo territory, where vast oil reserves are believed to exist. Seismic surveys conducted by both Guyana and Venezuela have provided valuable data on the geology and potential oil deposits in the region, fueling the desire to claim ownership of the area.

Extraction techniques have also evolved significantly, with the advent of more sophisticated drilling technologies. Horizontal drilling and hydraulic fracturing, commonly known as fracking, have made it possible to extract oil from previously inaccessible reserves. These techniques have been employed by oil companies operating in the Esequibo territory, further intensifying the dispute as both Guyana and Venezuela seek to exploit this valuable resource.

However, the environmental impact of such extraction techniques cannot be overlooked. Fracking, in particular, has raised concerns regarding water contamination and seismic activity. The subchapter will explore the potential consequences of these extraction methods on the fragile ecosystems and biodiversity of the Esequibo region, as well as the long-term sustainability of oil extraction in the area.

Moreover, the economic implications of the border dispute are closely intertwined with the technological advancements in oil extraction. The Esequibo territory is estimated to hold billions of barrels of oil, which has the potential to transform the economies of both Guyana and Venezuela. The subchapter will discuss the economic benefits and challenges associated with oil exploration and extraction, including the potential for wealth generation, job creation, and infrastructure development, as well as the risks of resource curse and economic dependence on oil.

Furthermore, the geopolitical factors influencing the border dispute cannot be ignored. The Esequibo territory's strategic location and its oil reserves have attracted the attention of global powers, adding a complex dimension to the dispute. The subchapter will explore the geopolitical interests of key players and how they influence the dynamics of the border dispute.

Finally, the subchapter will provide perspectives and opinions from local residents and stakeholders in the disputed area, giving voice to those directly affected by the ongoing conflict. Their insights will shed light on the social and cultural consequences of the dispute, as well as the impact on regional stability and relations between Guyana and Venezuela.

In summary, technological advancements and extraction techniques have not only fueled the border dispute between Guyana and Venezuela over the Esequibo oil-rich territory but have also raised important environmental, economic, geopolitical, and social considerations. Understanding the role of technology in this dispute is crucial for the public, as well as for those interested in the Guyana-Venezuela border dispute and its wider implications.

Economic and environmental considerations in oil production

The exploration and exploitation of oil resources in the Esequibo oil-rich territory is a topic that raises important economic and environmental considerations. This subchapter delves into the impact of oil production on the disputed Guyana-Venezuela border and the wider implications for both countries and the region.

From an economic perspective, the Esequibo oil-rich territory holds significant potential for both Guyana and Venezuela. The discovery of vast oil reserves has sparked interest from international oil companies, leading to increased investment and potential economic growth. However, the border dispute has created uncertainty and hindered the development of these resources. The legal aspects of the dispute affect the ability of Guyana to fully explore and exploit the oil reserves, limiting the economic benefits that could be derived from this resource.

Furthermore, the geopolitical factors influencing the border dispute also have economic implications. The tension between Guyana and Venezuela has deterred foreign direct investment and created a climate of uncertainty, which could discourage potential investors from entering the region. This not only affects the oil industry but also other sectors of the economy that are dependent on stable and secure international relations.

While the economic considerations are important, it is crucial not to overlook the environmental impact of oil production. The exploitation of oil resources can have severe consequences for the environment, including deforestation, habitat destruction, and water pollution. These impacts can have long-lasting effects on the ecosystems and biodiversity of the region, as well as the livelihoods of local communities who rely on these natural resources for their survival.

The subchapter also explores the social and cultural consequences of the dispute on affected communities. The border dispute has created divisions among communities living in the disputed area, causing social tensions and affecting cultural practices that have been passed down through generations. Additionally, the lack of clarity and resolution regarding the border dispute has left these communities in a state of uncertainty and vulnerability.

International mediation efforts have been made to resolve the border dispute, recognizing the potential for both economic and environmental harm. These efforts aim to find a peaceful and mutually beneficial solution that takes into account the interests of both Guyana and Venezuela, as well as the concerns of the international community.

Finally, the subchapter includes perspectives and opinions from local residents and stakeholders in the disputed area. Their voices provide valuable insights into the human impact of the border dispute and the importance of finding a resolution that considers both economic development and environmental preservation.

In conclusion, the economic and environmental considerations in oil production in the Esequibo oil-rich territory play a significant role in the ongoing Guyana-Venezuela border dispute. The subchapter explores the various aspects of this complex issue, highlighting the need for a balanced approach that takes into account the interests of both countries, the well-being of local communities, and the preservation of the environment.

International mediation efforts in resolving the border dispute

International mediation efforts have played a crucial role in the ongoing border dispute between Guyana and Venezuela over the Esequibo oil-rich territory. This subchapter explores the various initiatives taken by the international community to resolve this longstanding issue.

Since the colonial era, the border dispute between Guyana and Venezuela has remained a contentious issue. Both countries have staked their claims over the Esequibo region, which is believed to hold significant oil reserves. As the dispute escalated, international mediation efforts became essential to prevent further escalation and find a peaceful resolution.

The United Nations has been actively involved in mediating the border dispute. In 1966, the UN Secretary-General appointed a Good Offices Representative to facilitate negotiations between the two countries. Over the years, several Good Offices Representatives have been appointed, working closely with both governments to find common ground and reach a mutually acceptable solution.

Additionally, the International Court of Justice (ICJ) has played a significant role in the mediation process. In 2018, Guyana filed a case against Venezuela at the ICJ, seeking a legal resolution to the dispute. The court has jurisdiction to hear the case and will play a vital role in determining the validity of the border claims.

Regional organizations such as the Caribbean Community (CARICOM) and the Organization of American States (OAS) have also been engaged in mediating the dispute. These organizations have facilitated dialogue between Guyana and Venezuela, provided a platform for negotiations, and encouraged peaceful resolution through diplomatic channels.

The international mediation efforts have aimed to address not only the territorial claims but also the socio-economic and environmental implications of the dispute. The Esequibo region, known for its rich biodiversity, has suffered due to the uncertainty surrounding its ownership. The mediation efforts have sought to protect the environment and ensure sustainable development in the disputed area.

The resolution of the border dispute holds significant implications for regional stability and relations between Guyana and Venezuela. Resolving the dispute would contribute to a more conducive environment for cooperation and economic development in the region.

Local residents and stakeholders in the disputed area have expressed their perspectives and opinions on the matter. Their voices are crucial in understanding the social and cultural consequences of the dispute on affected communities. The international mediation efforts must consider these perspectives to ensure a fair and just resolution that addresses the concerns of all parties involved.

In conclusion, international mediation efforts have been instrumental in resolving the border dispute between Guyana and Venezuela. The involvement of the United Nations, the International Court of Justice, and regional organizations like CARICOM and the OAS has provided a platform for dialogue, negotiation, and a peaceful resolution. The outcome of these efforts will not only impact the disputed area but also regional stability, economic cooperation, and the environment. It is vital that the perspectives and opinions of local residents and stakeholders are considered throughout the mediation process to ensure a fair and inclusive resolution.

Role of international organizations and diplomatic initiatives

The role of international organizations and diplomatic initiatives in the Guyana-Venezuela border dispute and their claims over the Esequibo oil-rich territory is crucial in addressing the complex challenges and finding a peaceful resolution. This subchapter explores the various efforts made by international organizations and diplomatic initiatives to mediate and resolve the dispute, considering its historical background, legal aspects, environmental impact, economic implications, geopolitical factors, social and cultural consequences, exploration and exploitation of oil resources, impact on regional stability and relations between Guyana and Venezuela, as well as perspectives from local residents and stakeholders in the disputed area.

International organizations such as the United Nations (UN), Organization of American States (OAS), Caribbean Community (CARICOM), and others have played a significant role in facilitating dialogue and negotiations between Guyana and Venezuela. They have provided platforms for both countries to present their cases, exchange views, and seek a peaceful settlement. These organizations have also offered technical assistance and expertise to support the resolution process, including the demarcation of borders and legal advice.

Diplomatic initiatives have played a vital role in bridging the gap between the two nations. Diplomatic efforts by neighboring countries, regional powers, and other international actors have aimed to encourage dialogue, promote understanding, and foster trust between Guyana and Venezuela. Mediation efforts by countries like Norway and the United States have been instrumental in bringing the two nations to the negotiation table and facilitating productive discussions.

The impact of the border dispute on regional stability cannot be underestimated. It has strained relations between Guyana and Venezuela, affecting trade, investment, and regional cooperation. The involvement of international organizations and diplomatic initiatives has helped mitigate tensions and maintain stability in the region by promoting peaceful resolutions and discouraging any escalation of conflict.

Furthermore, the perspectives and opinions of local residents and stakeholders in the disputed area are crucial in understanding the human dimension of the dispute. Their voices shed light on the social and cultural consequences of the border dispute, including displacement, loss of livelihoods, and disruptions to local communities. It is imperative to consider their concerns and involve them in the resolution process to ensure a fair and just outcome.

In conclusion, international organizations and diplomatic initiatives have played a pivotal role in addressing the Guyana-Venezuela border dispute and the claims over the Esequibo oil-rich territory. Their efforts have focused on facilitating dialogue, providing technical assistance, mediating negotiations, and promoting regional stability. The involvement of local residents and stakeholders is essential to ensure a comprehensive and inclusive resolution that considers the social, cultural, and economic aspects of the dispute.

Analysis of past mediation attempts and their outcomes

The Guyana-Venezuela border dispute over the Esequibo oil-rich territory has been a long-standing issue with significant implications for both countries and the region. Over the years, several mediation attempts have been made to resolve the dispute and find a mutually acceptable solution. In this subchapter, we will analyze these past mediation efforts and their outcomes.

Historically, the border dispute between Guyana and Venezuela dates back to the 19th century when Venezuela claimed ownership of the Esequibo region. Since then, numerous international mediators, such as the United Nations and the Commonwealth, have been involved in facilitating negotiations between the two countries.

One of the most notable mediation processes took place under the auspices of the United Nations Secretary-General in the 1980s. The UN Good Offices Mission sought to bring both parties to the negotiating table and find a peaceful resolution. However, despite several rounds of talks, no consensus was reached, and the mediation efforts eventually stalled.

Another significant mediation attempt occurred in the early 2000s, when both countries agreed to engage in the Good Offices Process facilitated by the Secretary-General of the United Nations. This process included the appointment of a Personal Representative to explore possible solutions to the dispute. Unfortunately, these efforts also failed to yield a resolution, and the dispute remained unresolved.

The outcomes of these mediation attempts have had varying impacts on the region. On one hand, the failure to reach a resolution has led to increased tensions between Guyana and Venezuela, affecting regional stability and bilateral relations. The ongoing dispute has also hindered economic development in the Esequibo territory, as potential investors remain wary of investing in an area with unresolved ownership claims.

Moreover, the social and cultural consequences of the dispute have been significant for the affected communities. Local residents have been caught in the crossfire of the dispute, with their lives and livelihoods disrupted by the uncertainty surrounding the territory's ownership.

Despite the failures of past mediation attempts, the desire for a resolution remains strong among local residents and stakeholders in the disputed area. Their perspectives and opinions provide valuable insights into the human impact of the border dispute and the urgent need for a peaceful resolution.

In conclusion, the analysis of past mediation attempts reveals the complexities and challenges of resolving the Guyana-Venezuela border dispute. The outcomes of these efforts have had far-reaching implications for the region, affecting economic, social, and geopolitical factors. As the dispute continues to evolve, it is crucial to consider the lessons learned from past mediation attempts and explore new avenues for dialogue and compromise. Only through sustained and sincere efforts can a lasting resolution be achieved, bringing stability and prosperity to the affected communities and the region as a whole.

Prospects for future negotiations and potential resolutions

The Guyana-Venezuela border dispute over the Esequibo Oil-Rich Territory has been a longstanding issue that has affected both nations and their surrounding regions. As the public, it is important for us to understand the prospects for future negotiations and potential resolutions to this complex and multifaceted conflict.

Historically, the border dispute between Guyana and Venezuela can be traced back to the 19th century, when Venezuela claimed ownership over the Esequibo region. Despite various attempts at resolving the issue through diplomatic means, no concrete solution has been reached thus far. However, there is hope that future negotiations can bring about a peaceful resolution.

Legally, both countries have presented their arguments based on historical treaties and agreements. The International Court of Justice (ICJ) has been involved in the case since 2018, and its decision is expected to have a significant impact on the dispute. The court's ruling, expected in the near future, will provide a legal framework for potential resolutions.

Environmental concerns surrounding the Esequibo oil-rich territory are another crucial aspect of the dispute. Any resolution must take into account the preservation of the region's delicate ecosystem. Sustainable development and responsible exploitation of resources should be key considerations in future negotiations.

Economically, the border dispute has hindered the development of the Esequibo region, which is believed to hold substantial oil reserves. A resolution to the dispute would unlock the potential for economic growth and investment, benefiting both Guyana and Venezuela.

Geopolitically, the border dispute has implications beyond the two nations involved. Regional stability and relations between Guyana and Venezuela have been strained, affecting the wider Caribbean community. A peaceful resolution would contribute to regional cooperation and harmony.

The social and cultural consequences of the dispute on affected communities cannot be overlooked. The border dispute has created uncertainty and tension among residents in the disputed area. Their perspectives and opinions should be given due consideration in any negotiation and resolution process.

International mediation efforts have played a significant role in resolving the border dispute. The involvement of impartial third parties, such as the United Nations, has helped facilitate dialogue between Guyana and Venezuela. Continued support from the international community will be vital in reaching a fair and lasting resolution.

In conclusion, while the Guyana-Venezuela border dispute over the Esequibo Oil-Rich Territory remains unresolved, there are prospects for future negotiations and potential resolutions. The legal, environmental, economic, geopolitical, social, and cultural aspects of the dispute must be carefully considered in any negotiation process. With international support and a commitment to dialogue, a peaceful resolution that benefits all stakeholders involved can be achieved.

Impact of the border dispute on regional stability and relations between Guyana and Venezuela

The border dispute between Guyana and Venezuela has had a significant impact on regional stability and relations between the two nations. The ongoing conflict over the Esequibo oil-rich territory has created tensions and strained diplomatic ties, resulting in various consequences for both countries and the wider region.

At its core, the border dispute represents a clash of historical claims and legal interpretations. The roots of the conflict can be traced back to the colonial era, with both Guyana and Venezuela asserting their rights over the disputed territory. The legal aspects of the dispute have been complex, involving international arbitration and legal proceedings, further complicating the resolution process.

The environmental impact of the Esequibo oil-rich territory cannot be overlooked. The disputed area is home to diverse ecosystems and natural resources, which are at risk due to the exploration and exploitation of oil resources. The environmental consequences of such activities can have long-lasting effects on the region's biodiversity and ecosystems.

Economically, the border dispute has had implications for both Guyana and Venezuela. The Esequibo territory is believed to hold vast oil reserves, making it a valuable asset for any nation. The uncertainty surrounding the ownership of the territory has hindered investment and development potential, affecting the economic prospects of both countries.

Geopolitical factors have also played a significant role in the border dispute. The dispute has attracted the attention of other nations and international organizations, with various geopolitical interests at stake. These interests have influenced the dynamics of the conflict, further complicating efforts to reach a resolution.

The social and cultural consequences of the dispute have been felt by the affected communities living in the disputed area. The uncertainty and instability have disrupted their lives, causing displacement and anxiety. Moreover, the dispute has strained social and cultural ties between Guyana and Venezuela, impacting people's interactions and relationships.

International mediation efforts have been made to resolve the border dispute, but a definitive solution remains elusive. The impact of these efforts on regional stability is notable, as the unresolved conflict continues to create tension and uncertainty in the region.

Perspectives and opinions from local residents and stakeholders in the disputed area provide valuable insights into the human impact of the border dispute. These voices shed light on the lived experiences of those affected, giving a human face to the conflict and highlighting the urgency for a resolution.

In conclusion, the border dispute between Guyana and Venezuela has had far-reaching implications for regional stability and relations between the two nations. The conflict's impact on the environment, economy, geopolitics, and social fabric of the region cannot be understated. It is crucial for all stakeholders to work towards a peaceful resolution that addresses the concerns of all parties involved and ensures long-term stability and prosperity for the region.

Political tensions and their impact on regional cooperation

Political tensions between Guyana and Venezuela have had a significant impact on regional cooperation in the dispute over the Esequibo oil-rich territory. This subchapter explores the various dimensions of this issue and highlights the consequences it has had on different aspects of the region.

The historical background of the Guyana-Venezuela border dispute is a complex narrative that dates back to the colonial era. Both countries have claimed ownership over the Esequibo territory, leading to a prolonged conflict that has persisted for decades. The legal aspects of the dispute have been a subject of intense scrutiny, with international arbitration processes attempting to find a resolution.

The environmental impact of the Esequibo oil-rich territory cannot be ignored. The potential for oil exploration and exploitation in the region has raised concerns about environmental degradation and the loss of biodiversity. The fragile ecosystems of the area are at risk, and steps must be taken to ensure sustainable development practices are implemented.

Economically, the border dispute has had far-reaching implications. The uncertainty surrounding the ownership of the Esequibo territory has deterred foreign investment and hindered economic development in both countries. The dispute has also affected the fishing and mining industries, which are vital sources of income for local communities.

Geopolitical factors have played a significant role in perpetuating the border dispute between Guyana and Venezuela. The strategic importance of the Esequibo territory, coupled with the wider geopolitical interests of other nations, has complicated efforts to find a peaceful resolution.

The social and cultural consequences of the dispute have been felt by the affected communities. The uncertainty and tensions surrounding the border have disrupted the lives of residents, leading to a sense of insecurity and instability. Cultural exchanges and cooperation between the two nations have been strained, further exacerbating the divide.

International mediation efforts have been ongoing, with various organizations and countries attempting to facilitate a resolution. However, progress has been slow, and the dispute continues to impact regional stability and relations between Guyana and Venezuela. The potential for escalation and conflict remains a concern.

Local residents and stakeholders in the disputed area have diverse perspectives and opinions on the border dispute. Their voices must be heard and considered in any resolution process. Their livelihoods and future are at stake, and their input is crucial for any sustainable and just outcome.

In conclusion, the political tensions between Guyana and Venezuela have had far-reaching consequences on regional cooperation. The border dispute over the Esequibo territory has impacted various aspects of the region, including the environment, economy, geopolitics, and social fabric. Efforts must be made to find a peaceful resolution that takes into account the perspectives of local residents and stakeholders, while ensuring sustainable development and regional stability.

Border security and cross-border criminal activities

Border security is a pressing concern when it comes to cross-border criminal activities in the context of the Guyana-Venezuela border dispute and their claims over the Esequibo oil-rich territory. This subchapter aims to shed light on the various dimensions of this issue, exploring its historical background, legal aspects, environmental impact, economic implications, geopolitical factors, social and cultural consequences, exploration and exploitation of oil resources, international mediation efforts, and the perspectives and opinions of local residents and stakeholders.

The Guyana-Venezuela border dispute has a long and complex historical background, rooted in conflicting territorial claims dating back to the colonial era. This dispute has legal implications, as both countries have presented their cases before various international bodies, such as the United Nations and the International Court of Justice. The resolution of the dispute holds significant environmental consequences, as the Esequibo oil-rich territory is a region of great ecological value and biodiversity.

The economic implications of the border dispute are substantial, as the Esequibo territory is believed to hold vast oil and gas reserves. The control over these resources could greatly impact the economic development of both countries. Geopolitical factors also play a role in this dispute, as it involves regional and international players with vested interests in the outcome.

The social and cultural consequences of the dispute are felt by the affected communities living in the disputed area. These communities face uncertainty, displacement, and potential conflict, as their identities and ways of life are intertwined with the territory.

Exploration and exploitation of oil resources in the Esequibo territory are controversial due to the unresolved border dispute. International mediation efforts have been ongoing, with attempts to find a peaceful resolution through diplomatic channels and legal mechanisms.

The border dispute has implications for regional stability and relations between Guyana and Venezuela, as it creates tensions and impacts cooperation in various areas, such as trade and security.

To gain a comprehensive understanding of the issue, it is essential to consider the perspectives and opinions of local residents and stakeholders in the disputed area. Their voices provide insights into the human impact of the border dispute and the various interests at stake.

In conclusion, border security and cross-border criminal activities are significant aspects of the Guyana-Venezuela border dispute and their claims over the Esequibo oil-rich territory. This subchapter explores the multifaceted dimensions of this issue, highlighting its historical, legal, environmental, economic, geopolitical, social, and cultural aspects, as well as the exploration and exploitation of oil resources, international mediation efforts, and the perspectives of local residents and stakeholders.

Implications for regional integration and stability

The Guyana-Venezuela border dispute and the claims over the Esequibo oil-rich territory have far-reaching implications for regional integration and stability. This subchapter aims to explore the various aspects of this issue and shed light on its potential consequences.

Historically, the border dispute between Guyana and Venezuela has strained regional relations. The conflicting claims over the Esequibo territory have created tensions between the two countries, impacting their ability to collaborate and work towards regional integration. This ongoing dispute hampers the establishment of stable diplomatic relations and impedes efforts to foster economic cooperation and social development in the region.

From a legal perspective, the unresolved border dispute raises questions about the stability and reliability of established international norms and agreements. The dispute challenges the authority of international bodies, such as the United Nations, to enforce their decisions and mediate conflicts effectively. This undermines the credibility of international law and sets a dangerous precedent for future territorial disputes.

The environmental impact of the Esequibo oil-rich territory is another significant concern. The exploration and exploitation of oil resources in the disputed area could have severe ecological consequences, affecting the fragile ecosystems and biodiversity of the region. This poses a threat to the sustainable development goals of both Guyana and Venezuela and hinders their ability to address climate change and environmental challenges.

Economically, the border dispute has implications for both countries. The uncertainty surrounding the ownership of the Esequibo territory hinders foreign investment and economic development in the region. The potential wealth generated from the oil resources remains untapped, depriving both Guyana and Venezuela of significant economic opportunities. This lack of economic integration exacerbates existing socio-economic disparities and hampers regional stability.

Geopolitically, the border dispute influences the power dynamics within the region. The involvement of external actors, such as the United States, China, and Russia, further complicates the situation and adds to the geopolitical tensions. The border dispute becomes a geopolitical chessboard, with interests and alliances influencing the outcomes and potentially destabilizing the region.

Socially and culturally, the dispute has profound consequences for the affected communities. The uncertainty and tensions surrounding the border dispute have disrupted the lives of people living in the disputed area. Communities have been displaced, and their way of life has been upended. This has led to social and cultural disintegration, as communities struggle to maintain their identity and traditions amidst the turmoil.

Efforts at international mediation have been made to resolve the border dispute, but progress has been slow. The lack of a resolution perpetuates regional instability and strains the relations between Guyana and Venezuela. The dispute hampers cooperation and collaboration on regional issues, hindering the potential for regional integration and stability.

Local residents and stakeholders in the disputed area have diverse perspectives and opinions on the matter. Their voices and experiences must be taken into account in any resolution process. Engaging with these communities and understanding their concerns is essential for fostering regional integration and stability.

In conclusion, the implications of the Guyana-Venezuela border dispute and the claims over the Esequibo oil-rich territory are significant for regional integration and stability. The dispute affects various aspects, including historical, legal, environmental, economic, geopolitical, social, and cultural factors. Resolving the dispute is crucial for fostering regional cooperation, stability, and sustainable development.

Perspectives and opinions from local residents and stakeholders in the disputed area

In the subchapter titled "Perspectives and opinions from local residents and stakeholders in the disputed area," it is crucial to shed light on the voices of those directly affected by the Guyana-Venezuela border dispute and the claims over the Esequibo Oil-Rich Territory. By exploring the viewpoints of local residents and stakeholders, we can gain a deeper understanding of the complexities and nuances surrounding this contentious issue.

The perspectives and opinions from local residents and stakeholders in the disputed area are diverse and multifaceted. Many individuals have lived in the region for generations, witnessing the evolving dynamics of the border dispute and its impact on their lives. These individuals possess a wealth of knowledge and insights that are invaluable in comprehending the human aspect of the conflict.

For some local residents, the border dispute has created significant challenges. The uncertainty and tension surrounding the territorial claims have disrupted their daily lives, affecting their livelihoods, access to basic services, and infrastructure development. They express frustration and anxiety about the protracted nature of the dispute, fearing that a resolution may never be reached.

On the other hand, there are stakeholders who hold strong nationalist sentiments and firmly believe in their country's claims over the Esequibo territory. They argue that the oil-rich region belongs rightfully to their nation and perceive any compromise as a betrayal of their national identity. These individuals emphasize historical, legal, and geopolitical factors to support their position.

Interestingly, there are also local residents and stakeholders who advocate for peaceful dialogue and compromise. They emphasize the need for both Guyana and Venezuela to come together and find a mutually beneficial solution. These individuals underscore the potential for collaboration in resource exploration and economic development, which could bring prosperity to the region and improve the lives of its inhabitants.

Moreover, it is important to consider the perspectives of indigenous communities residing in the disputed area. These communities have a deep connection to the land and its resources, and their voices deserve particular attention. Their perspectives often prioritize environmental sustainability, cultural preservation, and the protection of their rights and ancestral territories.

By incorporating the perspectives and opinions of local residents and stakeholders, this subchapter aims to provide a comprehensive understanding of the human dimensions of the Guyana-Venezuela border dispute and the claims over the Esequibo Oil-Rich Territory. It highlights the complexities, aspirations, and concerns of those who have a direct stake in the resolution of this long-standing conflict.

Voices of affected communities and their experiences

The subchapter titled "Voices of affected communities and their experiences" sheds light on the lived experiences and perspectives of the communities directly impacted by the Guyana-Venezuela border dispute and their claims over the Esequibo oil-rich territory. This section aims to provide a platform for the public, as well as those interested in the Guyana-Venezuela border dispute and its implications, to hear the stories and opinions of local residents and stakeholders in the disputed area.

Within the disputed territory, communities have been grappling with the consequences of this unresolved dispute for generations. The experiences of these communities, often marginalized and overlooked, offer valuable insights into the social, cultural, economic, and environmental impacts of the ongoing border dispute.

Local residents recount the hardships they face due to the disputed status of the land they inhabit. They share stories of uncertainty, anxiety, and instability, as their lives are constantly influenced by the geopolitical factors at play. The lack of clear boundaries and ownership has led to conflicts and tensions within and between communities, affecting their social fabric.

Furthermore, the exploration and exploitation of oil resources in the Esequibo territory have had both positive and negative effects on the affected communities. Some locals express hope for economic prosperity and development, while others voice concerns about the potential environmental degradation and displacement of their communities.

The subchapter also presents the perspectives and opinions of stakeholders from both Guyana and Venezuela. These include government officials, indigenous leaders, environmental activists, and experts who have a vested interest in the border dispute. Their insights provide a comprehensive understanding of the multidimensional nature of the conflict and possible solutions to resolve it.

By amplifying the voices of affected communities and stakeholders, this subchapter aims to foster empathy, understanding, and engagement among the public. It encourages readers to critically examine the complexities of the border dispute and its far-reaching implications, highlighting the need for peaceful resolution and the importance of considering the perspectives and experiences of those directly impacted.

Ultimately, this section aims to contribute to the ongoing dialogue surrounding the Guyana-Venezuela border dispute and foster informed discussions on the way forward. It serves as a reminder that behind every geopolitical conflict, there are real people with real stories, whose lives are deeply affected by the decisions made by governments and international entities.

Views of government officials and local leaders

In the subchapter titled "Views of government officials and local leaders," we delve into the perspectives of those in positions of power and influence regarding the Guyana-Venezuela border dispute and the Esequibo oil-rich territory. These viewpoints reflect the complexities and nuances surrounding the issue, providing valuable insights into the ongoing dispute.

Government officials from both Guyana and Venezuela play a crucial role in shaping the narrative of the border dispute. Guyana's government officials staunchly defend their territorial integrity, emphasizing historical evidence and legal claims to support their stance. They argue that the 1899 Arbitral Award settled the border and that any attempts to challenge it are unjustified. Moreover, they highlight the economic potential of the Esequibo oil-rich territory, asserting that its development will benefit both nations.

On the other hand, Venezuelan government officials assert that the 1899 Arbitral Award was null and void, claiming that it was a result of coercion and imperialism. They maintain that the Esequibo region rightfully belongs to Venezuela and emphasize the importance of historical and cultural ties to the territory. Additionally, they argue that the exploitation of oil resources in the Esequibo is a violation of their sovereignty.

Local leaders in the disputed area provide a unique perspective, representing the voices of the affected communities. They often express concerns about the potential environmental and social consequences of oil exploration and exploitation. These leaders advocate for inclusive dialogue and peaceful resolution of the border dispute to ensure the well-being of their communities.

While government officials and local leaders have varying opinions, they all recognize the geopolitical factors at play in the border dispute. They acknowledge the potential impact on regional stability and relations between Guyana and Venezuela, highlighting the need for diplomatic solutions and international mediation.

The views of government officials and local leaders shed light on the multi-faceted nature of the border dispute and its implications. Their perspectives contribute to a comprehensive understanding of the issue, enabling the public and stakeholders to engage in informed discussions and support peaceful resolution efforts.

Insights from experts and scholars on the ground

In the subchapter titled "Insights from experts and scholars on the ground," we delve into the valuable perspectives offered by individuals who have dedicated their research and expertise to understanding the complexities of the Guyana-Venezuela border dispute and the Esequibo Oil-Rich Territory. Their insights shed light on various aspects of the dispute, including its historical background, legal aspects, environmental impact, economic implications, geopolitical factors, social and cultural consequences, exploration and exploitation of oil resources, international mediation efforts, and the impact on regional stability and relations between Guyana and Venezuela.

Historical Background of the Guyana-Venezuela Border Dispute:

Experts and scholars provide a comprehensive historical overview of the dispute, tracing its roots back to the colonial era and examining the different historical claims made by both Guyana and Venezuela. They highlight key events and agreements that have shaped the dispute over the years, providing a deeper understanding of the historical context.

Legal Aspects of the Guyana-Venezuela Border Dispute:

Legal experts analyze the relevant international laws, treaties, and agreements that govern territorial disputes, such as the Geneva Agreement of 1966. They explore the legal arguments presented by both countries and offer their interpretations on the legal implications of the dispute.

Environmental Impact of the Esequibo Oil-Rich Territory:

Environmental specialists discuss the potential environmental consequences of oil exploration and exploitation in the Esequibo territory. They examine the risks associated with oil spills, deforestation, and habitat destruction, and explore sustainable alternatives that could mitigate these impacts.

Economic Implications of the Guyana-Venezuela Border Dispute:

Economists analyze the potential economic benefits and drawbacks for both Guyana and Venezuela in resolving the border dispute. They explore how the ownership of the Esequibo oil-rich territory could impact the economies of both countries, including the potential for increased investment, job creation, and economic development.

Geopolitical Factors Influencing the Border Dispute:

Scholars specializing in geopolitics discuss the broader regional and international factors that influence the Guyana-Venezuela border dispute. They analyze how geopolitical alliances, strategic interests, and power dynamics shape the positions of other countries and international organizations involved in the mediation efforts.

Social and Cultural Consequences of the Dispute on Affected Communities:

Experts in sociology and anthropology examine the social and cultural consequences of the border dispute on the communities living in the disputed area. They explore the impact on indigenous populations, the displacement of communities, and the erosion of cultural heritage.

Exploration and Exploitation of Oil Resources in the Esequibo Territory:

Energy experts provide insights into the technical challenges and opportunities associated with oil exploration and exploitation in the

Esequibo territory. They discuss the potential reserves, the feasibility of extraction, and the economic viability of developing the oil resources in the disputed area.

International Mediation Efforts in Resolving the Border Dispute:

Scholars specializing in international relations and diplomacy analyze the various mediation efforts undertaken by regional and international actors to resolve the Guyana-Venezuela border dispute. They assess the effectiveness of these efforts and explore potential avenues for successful mediation.

Impact of the Border Dispute on Regional Stability and Relations between Guyana and Venezuela:

Experts in international security and political science examine the impact of the border dispute on regional stability and the bilateral relations between Guyana and Venezuela. They analyze the potential escalation of tensions, the implications for peace and security in the region, and the role of diplomacy in preventing conflicts.

Perspectives and Opinions from Local Residents and Stakeholders in the Disputed Area:

The subchapter concludes by incorporating the perspectives and opinions of local residents and stakeholders living in the disputed area. Their voices provide an invaluable grassroots perspective on the impact of the border dispute on their lives, livelihoods, and aspirations for the future.

Overall, this subchapter offers a comprehensive analysis of the Guyana-Venezuela border dispute and the Esequibo Oil-Rich Territory, drawing on the insights and expertise of experts and scholars on the ground. By examining various dimensions of the dispute, it aims to provide the public with a nuanced understanding of this complex issue and its far-reaching consequences.